GARDEN PONDS

BY DR. HERBERT R. AXELROD

INTRODUCTION

There are two basic reasons that people have a water garden. They either like the colorful fishes which can be maintained and bred in a garden pond, or they like the flowers of aquatic and margin plants. Of course you can have both plants and fishes, but either has to be the major reason for the pond. If you want plants to be your main theme, then accommodating the plants to make easy access to the water is not a strong concern.

If you want the main emphasis of your pond to be fishes, then the plants must be used to enhance the beauty of your garden pond without hindering you from visiting your pond fishes for feeding, breeding, training (to feed from your hand) and removal (when you get too many). Fishes seem to do better in ponds with live aquatic plants, especially submerged plants like *Anacharis, Elodea, Cabomba* and *Myriophyllum.*

This book is about fishes for the garden pond, with information about how to make a fish pond as beautiful as possible.

What are Quarterlies?

Because Garden Pond keeping is growing at a rapid pace, information on their selection, care and setup is vitally needed in the marketplace. Books, the usual way information of this sort is transmitted, can be too slow. Sometimes by the time a book is written and published, the material contained therein is a year or two old...and no new material has been added during that time. Only a book in a magazine form can bring breaking stories and current information. A magazine is streamlined in production, so we have adopted certain magazine publishing techniques in the creation of this Quarterlies. Magazines also can be produced much cheaper than books because they are supported by advertising. To combine these assets into a great publication, we issued this Quarterly in both magazine and book format at different prices.

Distributed in the UNITED STATES to the Pet Trade by T.F.H. Publications, Inc., One T.F.H. Plaza, Neptune City, NJ 07753; distributed in the UNITED STATES to the Bookstore and Library Trade by National Book Network, Inc. 4720 Boston Way, Lanham MD 20706; in CANADA to the Pet Trade by H & L Pet Supplies Inc., 27 Kingston Crescent, Kitchener, Ontario N2B 2T6; Rolf C. Hagen Inc., 3225 Sartelon St. Laurent-Montreal Quebec H4R 1E8; in CANADA to the Book Trade by Vanwell Publishing Ltd., 1 Northrup Crescent, St. Catharines, Ontario L2M 6P5 ; in ENGLAND by T.F.H. Publications, PO Box 15, Waterlooville PO7 6BQ; in AUSTRALIA AND THE SOUTH PACIFIC by T.F.H. (Australia), Pty. Ltd., Box 149, Brookvale 2100 N.S.W., Australia; in NEW ZEALAND by Brooklands Aquarium Ltd. 5 McGiven Drive, New Plymouth, RD1 New Zealand; in Japan by T.F.H. Publications, Japan—Jiro Tsuda, 10-12-3 Ohjidai, Sakura, Chiba 285, Japan; in SOUTH AFRICA by Lopis (Pty) Ltd., P.O. Box 39127, Booysens, 2016, Johannesburg, South Africa. Published by T.F.H. Publications, Inc.
MANUFACTURED IN THE
UNITED STATES OF AMERICA
BY T.F.H. PUBLICATIONS, INC.

Quarterly

yearBOOKS,INC.

Dr. Herbert R. Axelrod,
Founder & Chairman

Neal Pronek
Chief Editor

yearBOOKS and Quarterlies are all photo composed, color separated and designed on Scitex equipment in Neptune, N.J. with the following staff:

DIGITAL PRE-PRESS
Michael L. Secord
Supervisor
Robert Onyrscuk
Jose Reyes

COMPUTER ART
Thomas J. Ceballos
Patti Escabi
Sandra Taylor Gale
Candida Moreira
Joanne Muzyka
P. Northrup
Francine Shulman

Advertising Sales
George Campbell
Chief
Amy Manning
Director

©yearBOOKS,Inc.
1 TFH Plaza
Neptune, N.J. 07753
Completely manufactured in Neptune, N.J. USA

CONTENTS

The author's pond, filled with fishes, and more than 20 years old! Photo by Gary Hersch.

Ponds Suitable For Keeping Fishes

Not all bodies of water are suitable for maintaining fishes. In order to keep fishes alive and healthy in a garden pond, the pond must have suitable conveniences to keep it from over-heating, freezing solid, free of major algae growth, free of predatory animals and birds, and accessible to visual inspection and feeding. These concerns are the MINIMUM requirements. They are life and death subjects. If they are not addressed properly, the life of the fishes will be threatened.

OVER-HEATING

Small, shallow garden ponds, especially those made from vinyl sheeting, are prone to over-heating. When the vinyl is black, it becomes heated by the sun. The heat is driven into the water where, if it reaches a critical temperature, can kill the fish. Temperatures which reach the 90°F. mark are considered dangerous. Not only will the high temperatures create biological problems, but high temperatures usually mean lower oxygen content. Without sufficient oxygen in the water, fishes start to die. When you find a few dead fish floating in your pond, without apparent reason, you can usually trace it to a period of over-heating. Algae blooms, evidenced by pea-soup pond coloration, can be deadly to fishes when the water temperature rises above 82°F.

When you are concerned about your pond over-heating, there are two first-

A typical small water garden featuring fishes and plants. This was a home-made job using vinyl plastic sheeting. Photo by Dr. Burt Frank.

aid remedies recommended. The best remedy is to take a garden hose and aim it into the air so that the water will fall onto the surface of the pond creating as much turmoil as possible. This will both cool off the water and re-oxygenate it.

The second and less satisfactory method is to use a fountain. It is less satisfactory because it takes time to organize unless the pond is already equipped with one. With the pump usually lying on the bottom of the pond, debris almost always clogs up the fountain to some degree. Constant use will keep it operating, but the need for a huge surge of constant, fresh water is beyond the capability of in-pond fountains.

For severe emergencies, huge blocks of ice can be dropped into the pool to bring the temperature down quickly. This is not recommended because you might not have control of how thrive and breed at temperatures between 55° and 70°F. But they are not tolerant of rapid temperature fluctuations. Temperature variations of 10°F. up or down within any given 24 hour period are about the maximum temperature

Below: **This is a formal garden pond which only features fishes. There are very few water plants. Photo by Hugh Nicholas.**

Facing page: **A fine fishing line of nylon is used to hold the water hyacinth at one end of the pond. This is useful for the spawning fishes as well as the small fry. Photo by Dr. Burt Frank.**

low you want the temperature to drop. Most pond fishes like goldfish and koi can't take huge fluctuations of water temperature. They do well at water temperatures between 33° and 88°F., though they change to which most pond fishes can adapt. It is usually impossible to keep shallow, small outdoor water gardens within that temperature variation.

As there are tropical water lilies which perish when the

In the photo above, we see a pond which has frozen solid. This is very dangerous for the pond fishes as they have no air/water interface which allows for re-oxygenation of the water. If the pond freezes solid, the fish will be killed. In the pond below, water is bubbled under the surface to keep ice from forming. Photo by Dr. Burt Frank.

water becomes too cold, so are there tropical fishes like Mollies, Platies, Swordtails and Guppies which are also temperature sensitive. Yet a garden pond which can be maintained between 60°F. and 85°F. for a few months is ideal for some of the very colorful tropical fishes which are available at most pet shops.

FREEZING SOLID

If you live in an area where temperatures drop below freezing, and stay low enough for ponds to freeze, you have a problem. Fishes cannot live in ponds which freeze solid. They can, however, live quite comfortably in ponds which only freeze on the surface and the water under the ice is deep enough for the fishes to swim and maintain their normal swimming posture.

If you have doubts about your pond freezing solid, there are many procedures for protecting your fishes. Your local pet shop usually has submergible heaters, either in the form of an aquarium heater, or as a cable. The cables are used for outdoor water bowls for dogs (or farm animals). Another method is to cover the pond with a clear plastic sheet. This will form a greenhouse of sorts and the water will

Opposite page: **A beautiful series of connected ponds. The water runs from one pond to the other. One pond serves as aeration with a water pump. One pond is used for the fry. The main pond has lovely water lilies and large fishes.**

retain the sun's heat sufficiently to keep the water from freezing.

Running a fountain often is enough to keep a pond from freezing. As with over-heating, if a pond starts to freeze and you are concerned about it freezing solid, running a hose with water above 40°F. can usually assist the pond in staying warm enough not to freeze.

If your pond is very deep, say more than 3 feet deep, it is hardly likely that it will

ALGAE

For many years the plague of the water garden was the algae bloom which turned pond water pea-soup green. Many filters were devised and the only successful filters were those which were almost as large as the pool itself. Japanese koi magazines and books featured new ideas for pond filtration in every issue. 95% of the work involved with a koi pond had to do with the filtration system.

kill the algae, and many disease organisms as well. At the end of the UV tubes is a woven filter which has fine pores which enable it to capture the killed (and still

***Below:* This pond has a pump with a built in heater. It keeps the top of the pond free of ice all winter. Most aquarium shops can order this pump/heater combination for you. Photo by Dr. Burt Frank.**

freeze solid unless you live in normally frigid zones where frozen lakes are commonplace.

***Facing page:* If a pond is not protected from the sun with filtration and floating plants, it turns pea-soup green/brown and the fishes are hidden from view.**

Now all of that has changed. An American firm has invented and produced a small filter that removes the algae from any man-made pond in a few days. The filter is a series of ultra-violet lights in sealed tubes. There is a small pump which sucks or pushes the water through the tubes so the water is exposed to the UV light. The lighting is strong enough to

living) algae. The woven filter slips quickly on and off the tube and changing the filter is a matter of a few minutes. The woven filter is then washed and used again and again. For ponds heavily polluted with algae, the process might take three days, and depends on how religiously the filter is changed. But the filters are extraordinarily effective and

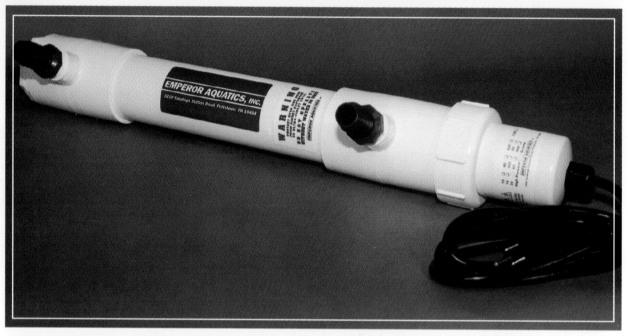

Ultraviolet germicidal energy is superior for killing algae, bacteria and protozoa exposed to its rays. The radiation reaches the DNA of the organisms, causing abrupt modification which brings about their swift destruction. For complete information about the UV filters, write to Emperor Aquatics, Inc., 2229 Sanatoga Station Road, Pottstown, Pa 194464 (phone (610) 970-0440). The author highly recommends this product for keeping your garden pond clear of algae.

much, much cheaper than the usual mechanical filters. Every garden pond must be equipped with UV filtration.

These filters have another feature. Last winter in New Jersey, we had record low temperatures. Ponds that never froze solid were doing just that. The UV filters were turned on and they generated enough heat to keep the ponds from freezing solid.

PREDATORY ANIMALS AND BIRDS

The larger and more natural your pond looks, the more likely you are to be victimized. There isn't very much you can do to protect your pond against snakes, frogs and other amphibians and reptiles. These animals are usually very small and cannot possibly capture and

eat a fish over 6 inches. Snakes are usually visible swimming on the top of the water. If you live in the country and can catch the snake with a noose, just cart it far away and release it in a natural setting. If they are a real problem, you might ask your local veterinary surgeon for names of people who might remove the snakes for you.

Many birds eat fishes, but the really dangerous birds are the herons. Some of the herons reach 5-6 feet in height and they wait by the side of the pond for an unsuspecting fish to swim by. There are few ways to protect your fishes. Wire mesh over the entire pond might help, but this is costly, difficult and stops your fishes from coming to the surface to

feed. By taking advantage of the heron's polite manners, you might rid yourself of them. If one heron visits your pond daily, it is doubtful that another heron will come. Many garden shops offer plastic herons. These are placed at the water's edge, but in the open so a visiting heron can see it from the air. Usually they will not come to visit since they respect the fishing rights of the heron already at your pond's edge.

Most of the other birds, like ducks and geese do not usually eat fishes. They prefer to munch on the

Facing page: The inner garden of the Meiji Shrine in Japan, features koi, turtles and water lilies. Photo by Roloff Beny.

Top: **Most outdoor ponds attract frogs or toads. They can only eat very small fishes or fish eggs. Their croaking can be pleasant or annoying depending upon your individual tastes.** *Middle:* **Sea gulls are fish eaters. If you live by the sea or by a large lake which is frequented by sea gulls, you should be aware of the problem.**

tender water lilies and other plants accessible to them. By placing a fence around your pond in which an aggressive dog or cat is confined the birds will surely stay away.

Other animals like dogs, cats, raccoons, foxes and even bears, often attack the fishes in the garden pond. Usually fenced in ponds keep these animals away.

Large ponds attract children who like to fish. A polite sign is usually all that it takes to discourage them from fishing. In more stubborn cases, a call to the local police surely will solve the problem.

VISIBLE INSPECTION AND FEEDING

The easiest symptom to recognize is a behavioral change in your fishes' feeding habits. You should feed your fishes from the same place at the same time every day. If the fishes are young (under 3 inches for koi), they can be

Bottom: **By using a plastic heron close to your pond, you will effectively keep living herons away from eating your pond fishes.**

Top: Large herons are catastrophic. They can eat koi up to a foot long. They can be kept away using a plastic heron decoy.

fed two or three times a day. In a few days, they should become accustomed to being fed and they should voraciously attack the floating food pellets. Koi have mouths which open towards the bottom of their bodies. They were *designed* to feed from the bottom. Now you are feeding them from the top. It may take a few days for them to get accustomed to this change.

If the fishes, once having become trained to attack the floating pellets, do not rise to the surface immediately upon being fed, there is a problem. Sometimes the problem is as simple as over-feeding. To judge how much to feed your fishes, just throw a few pellets onto the pond's surface at a time. When the fish stop eating voraciously, you'll know that you have reached the limit of their daily feeding. By feeding them from a measuring cup, you can ascertain exactly the quantity of food to offer every day. Of course, as the fishes grow, their appetites grow along with them.

Middle: Bears are voracious fish eaters. If you live where bears range, be aware of the problem. Bottom: Fish eating bats are dangerous because they attack the fishes at night when neither you nor the fish can see them.

Many water birds are attracted to your garden pond. In instances where your fishes are large and the birds are small, the birds' visits can be entertaining.

Raccoons and other predatory animals often fish in your pond and, when they fall in, are often found drowned. They can be kept out with a fencing system, most of which are expensive and ugly.

Foods and Feeding

This could be a very short chapter if you only keep adult koi in your pond. Feed them as much as they will eat in 3 minutes. Feed them every day as close to the same time as possible. Feed them floating pellets made especially for koi.

Note that adult koi have spawning periods, usually when the temperature rises close to 60°F. Below 50°F. they usually stop eating, though goldfish continue eating almost regardless of the water temperature. When they are spawning, they will, of course, eat their normal diet. But once they spawn and the fry appear, the diet must be changed. In order to keep the adults from preying on their own fry, you have to keep them from being hungry. This means that they must be fed as frequently as possible, but only as much as they consume in 3 minutes. The more frequently you feed the adults, the safer are the fry.

When the fry reach about one inch in size, they too must be fed. Usually the same pellets offered to the adults are ground into a fine powder with grains about half the size of rice. As the fry get larger, the pellets can be made larger.

***Facing page:* In Ritsurin Park, Takamatsu Shikoku features a huge garden pond. Visitors using the bridge can see the koi and even feed them floating pellets. Photo by Roloff Beny.**

Evelyn, the author's wife, has trained the koi to stick their head out of the water to take pellets from her hand. Photo by the author.

KINDS OF FOOD

Unfortunately, there are many so-called *koi* foods which are merely re-packaged dog, cat, trout or catfish pellets. Essentially there is nothing wrong in feeding your large koi some of these pellets, but usually they contain too much animal fat and eventually your koi will develop a fatty liver disease which is fatal. Hoping that the label on the package is honest, get the koi food with the lowest fat and with protein between 25 and 30%. With living plants in the pond, the koi will get extra nourishment by policing the bottom of the pond.

We only speak here about koi, but what we say about koi is also applicable to goldfish. Native fishes, even small trout and other easily acquired cold water species, also feed well on koi pellets. Trout and catfish do better on a koi pellet diet than koi do on a trout or catfish diet. The trout and catfish diet is designed to fatten the fish up as quickly as possible so they can be marketed as food. Koi diets encourage slow steady growth. The older and larger a koi is, the more valuable it becomes.

PELLET CHARACTERISTICS

You cannot tell how good a pellet is just by looking at it. It is best to test the pellet before you offer it to your pond fishes. Take a clear 8 oz. drinking glass and put in about 15 pellets. Make sure that ALL OF THEM FLOAT. If some pellets sink to the bottom of the glass, don't buy the food. What might happen is that the fish satisfy their hunger feeding from the surface. Those pellets which fall to the bottom may be uneaten. They will fall apart and feed the bacteria and other animalcules which cause cloudy water conditions. Cloudy water is dreadful. Not only does it have an obnoxious odor, but it may also kill all the fish in the pond. The only way to save the fish is to change as much of the water as possible with hoses directly from the tap. You can safely change 25% of the water in a given pond every day without endangering the fishes PROVIDING the water is approximately the same temperature as the water in the pond. A variation of 5°F. is acceptable.

Once you've tested the koi pellets for flotation, you now have to test for cleanliness. Pour out half the water in the glass. Allow the pellets to soak for about 5 minutes. Then put your hand over the top of the glass and shake the water vigorously. Much of each pellet should be dissolved and become heavier than water. It should sink. This is acceptable BUT the water must not be discolored. If the water is cloudy or colored, the food is bound together with starches or adhesives which may pollute your garden pond. Keep testing until you find the correct pellet. It's quite possible that you won't find a pellet which is 100% satisfactory. In this case, buy the best pellet possible...but keep looking as new pellets arrive onto the pet shop's shelf.

DO NOT ACCEPT ANY PELLET WHICH DOESN'T FLOAT. There is no sure way to measure your fish's appetites other than observing them while they eat.

GREEN FOODS

As you will soon learn, most koi, goldfish and other pond fishes enjoy fresh green leafy vegetables. Your water lilies, for example, will start sprouting about the same time the koi start eating. That's when the water temperature rises over the 50°F. mark. As the soft, tender shoots protrude from the bowls containing the water lilies, the fishes will eat them. It is very difficult to stop them from doing this, but there are some ways that can be suggested.

Take the outer leaves from heads of lettuce and scald them for a minute by pouring boiling water over them. Tear the leaves up into pieces a few inches in their maximum dimension and cast them onto the surface of the pond. They certainly will be eaten, but probably not while you are watching because they expect you to be broadcasting pellets and not vegetables! Be assured that the lettuce leaves will disappear in a few days. When the leaves disappear it will be time to replenish the supply. This MIGHT keep the koi and goldfish from devouring the tender new shoots of the water lilies.

A sure-fire way to protect the water lily from attack it to cover it with a wire basket. This will make the leaves a bit tougher to eat. Koi and goldfish can only eat the tips of the sprouts. They cannot bite into the stem once the leaf floats, so as soon as a leaf forms on the stem, the

Above: One of the great pleasures of having a fish pond is the ability to train the koi to be real pets. They are easily trained to eat from your hand. Photo by Hugh Nicholas.

Koi and goldfish are so popular as fish for outdoor ponds (with goldfish being popular also for indoor aquaria) that a number of manufacturers have made foods specifically formulated to feed to pool-dwelling koi and goldfish. Some of those foods are visible here in this view of many different fish foods marketed by Hikari USA. Photo courtesy Hikari USA.

goldfish and koi will ignore it. Your pet shop has protective baskets, or you can make your own. The basket should have as much space for growth as possible.

LIVE AND FROZEN FOODS

Unlike many fishes, neither koi nor goldfish have predatory teeth to catch and grasp living fishes for food. They might readily eat a small fish which they can swallow without chewing, but they usually don't hunt or pursue other fishes, even if they are small. They will, however, eat fish eggs, even their own! So when the koi or goldfish are spawning, you have to be sure there are lots of dense vegetation in which the eggs can be hidden from the adult fishes.

There are some live foods which are savored by koi and goldfish. The most readily available are small sewer worms called *Tubifex* worms. They are a staple diet for aquarium fishes. You can offer these to your pond fishes as a treat. They should be served in a large soup bowl. The bowl is put into the water first, without the worms. Then the worms are dropped in. The fish will eat them. The worms which get out of the bowl will become hidden in the debris on the bottom of the pond where they will breed and eventually be eaten by the koi and goldfish since these are bottom feeding fishes anyway.

Aquarium shops usually have a great selection of frozen foods. Usually these were once living animals but are seasonal in nature, so they are frozen. There are such frozen foods as insect larvae, *Daphnia,* beef heart which has been ground up, liver, clams, shrimp and salmon roe. Koi and goldfish will eat these things if they become accustomed to eating either from the soup bowl mentioned above, or from your hand.

HAND FEEDING

One of the great joys of keeping koi is that they become tame. The first step in their taming is learning to take food from your hand. Once the fish have become accustomed to feeding from the surface of the water, you can start the hand feeding studies. Take a handful of pellets and put your hand into the water with your fist tightly clenched. Once your hand is submerged and the fish seem to be curious, allow a few pellets to be released. As the pellets float away from your hand, the fish will eat them. They will slowly become braver until finally one or two will rush over to your hand and gobble mouthfuls of pellets. This has to be done on a daily basis for it to become standard feeding procedure, but it allows you to offer your fish treats such as the frozen foods mentioned above.

Once your fish have lost fear of your hand, you can now stroke them gently with your other hand whilst they are feeding. They might become startled and jump away, but slowly they will become accustomed to the petting.

The final phase of the hand feeding training is where the koi actually sticks its head *out of the water* begging for food. This is done by allowing a few pellets to drop from your hand while your hand is slightly above the water. The fish will soon learn to reach for the pellets...especially when they are hungry, so don't feed them for a day or two if they are reluctant to learn this behavior.

Your sprouting water lily can be protected from nibbling fishes by covering it with a wire basket. Photo by Joseph V. Tomocik.

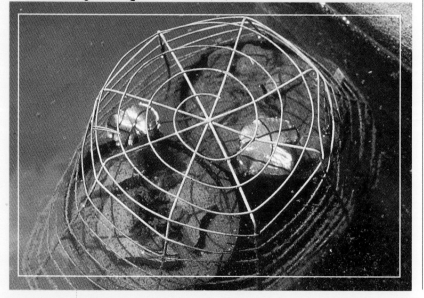

***Facing page:* Imagine the fun and pleasure when your hand is attacked by a group of hungry koi all sticking their heads out of the water! Photo by Hugh Nicholas.**

Plants for the Fish Pond

There are four basic kinds of plants with which to decorate your fish pond. Those plants which grow underwater and rarely emerge except to place their flowers where insects might visit them are called SUBMERGED plants. The principal plants found under this heading will be those common to most aquariums. Certainly *Cabomba*, *Anacharis*, *Elodea* and *Myriophyllum* are the best known examples of submerged plants.

Another kind of plant are those which FLOAT on the surface of the water, with their roots hanging into the water itself. The major plants in this category might be the Water Hyacinth and the Water Lettuce. There are many small floating plants which are collectively known as *duckweeds* because ducks are supposed to favor them. *Riccia* and *Lemna* are the two genera which are usually available through most aquarium stores, though there are many others. Frequently submerged plants are torn loose from their bases and float on the surface.

The WATER LILIES are the major group of plants popular with fish hobbyists because they are large, beautiful, hardy and inexpensive. Along with water lilies are the lotuses, but lotuses are shunned because they grow too aggressively and are difficult to eradicate once they have a foothold.

The final group of plants of interest to fish pond lovers

Above: **The author's pond in which koi are spawned and raised. Photo by the author.** *Below:* **In the winter, your pond can be covered over with a double plastic tent to keep it warm and flowering. Tropical plants and fishes can be a feature of the covered pond (but you will require space heaters,too).**

Above: The famous botanist and photographer Joseph V. Tomocik took this photo of his water garden in the Denver Botanical Gardens.

are the MARGINAL plants. These are flowering plants which are placed very close to the pond without actually being in it. The most familiar of these plants is the iris. Frequently iris are planted in waterproof clay pots and placed in the pond where the water is shallow enough so it doesn't enter the pot. Many other flowering plants can be utilized in the same manner.

SUBMERGED PLANTS

Your local pet store will have many varieties of submerged plants to sell you. In most cases they are tropical varieties of plants which you might find in your local stream or pond. DON'T USE THE PLANTS WHICH YOU MIGHT COLLECT IN LOCAL WATERS. The main reason for not using local plants is that they almost always contain parasites which prey upon fishes. They might even contain the eggs of frogs,salamanders or newts which, when they hatch, could be predatory on the fry of your goldfish or koi.

Most of the submerged plants are sold in bunches held together with a rubber band or a soft piece of lead. The lead is used so the plants do not float when the bunch is dropped into the tank or pond. By far the most popular of these bunch plants is *Anacharis,* also known as *Elodea.* These are very soft leafed plants which the goldfish and koi will enjoy tearing apart. They are especially valuable during the Spring spawning period when dozens of bunches are loosely tied together inviting the spawning fishes to use them as a spawning medium. After spawning, the plants can be retrieved with many of the eggs still adhering to them. Of course koi and goldfish eggs are not very adhesive so many of the eggs will fall to the bottom of the pond where they will either hatch or be eaten. There are other bunch plants which have tougher leaves.

Myriophyllum and *Ceratophyllum* are also sold in bunches and they can usually withstand the random picking of the fishes because their leaves are tough. *Cabomba* which looks something like *Myriophyllum* has a softer leaf and,

Above: Nymphaea 'lucida' **shown as a multitude of blossoms. This hardy wa-ter lily is shown at the Denver Botanical Gardens. Photo by Joseph V. Tomocik.** *Below:* **A magnificent multitude of blossoms from the hardy wa-ter lily** *Nymphaea* 'Darwin' **or** 'Hollandia' **produced by Latour-Marliac. Photo by Joseph V. Tomocik.**

The 'Bateau' water lily.

The 'Rosita' water lily.

The 'Berthol' water lily.

The 'Lucida' water lily.

The 'Princess Elizabeth' water lily.

The 'Solfatare' water lily.

The 'Charles de Meurville' water lily.

The 'Tulipformis' water lily.

The 'Madame Maurice Laydecker' water lily.

The 'Comte de Bouchard' water lily.

The 'Rose Magnolia' water lily.

Drawings by Candida Moreira after R.G.A. Davies' book *IDENTIFICATION OF HARDY NYMPHAEA* issued by the International Water Lily Society. This huge, magnificent series is available from Stapely Water Gardens.

Above: Nymphaea 'Rosy Morn', one of the world's outstanding pink hardy water lilies. Photo by Joseph V. Tomocik. Below: Nymphaea marliacia 'Chromatela', a very popular, hardy and reliable yellow water lily. Photo by Joseph V. Tomocik.

Above: Nymphaea 'Green Smoke'. Photo by Joseph V. Tomocik. *Below: Nymphaea* 'Mrs. George C. Hitchcock' is a tropical night blooming water lily developed by Pring. Photo by Joseph V. Tomocik.

Nymphaea zenkeri, a beautiful natural water lily. From Holger Windelov's Tropical Catalogue.

Barclaya longifolia is an excellent tropical plant for the shallows of the garden pond.

therefore, doesn't do as well as *Myriophyllum.*

All submerged plants can be purchased rooted in a small plastic pot. THESE ARE BY FAR THE BEST PLANTS. Simply place them into larger pots and allow them to grow luxuriously. Because these are usually tropical varieties, they will die when the water becomes too cold for them. Simply lift the pot and remove the plants and wait until the following Spring to re-plant them.

All of the bunch plants we have mentioned do have tiny flowers when everything goes their way. If their new growth is eaten by the fishes, they will not flower. It doesn't really matter because the flowers are very small and can hardly be cut and used as a decoration in your home. If you get very friendly with your water garden supplier, he might be able to get you locally bred bunch plants which can survive the winter in your pond.

FLOATING PLANTS

Duckweed, a name usually applied to any small plant which thrives and floats on a closed body of water like a lake or artificial pond, can be any one of many species of water plant.

The most common duckweed is the genus *Lemna.* These plants are found all over the world because ducks and geese unwittingly carry them around from one body of water to the next. The water fowl lands on a lake or pond, floats around for a while, getting bits of duckweed attached to its feathers, then flies off carrying the duckweed with it. Duckweed reproduces by lateral budding and, when conditions are right, huge quantities of duckweed are produced. In many situations, especially in the hydroponic culture of aquarium plants, the duckweed is a menace as it clogs up the pumps and lines carrying the nutrient solution to the roots of the plants being cultivated.

Many fishes eat duckweed, especially koi and goldfish. Should you add some temporary inhabitants to your pond, *Tilapia* with its many species (perhaps as many as 50!), thrives on duckweed and other plants and usually grows large enough in a season to be suitable for a barbecue. *Tilapia*, originating in Africa but now spread world-wide in the tropics, are major producers of protein for third world countries (nearly all of which are in the tropics!).

If you can only get a few small plants, don't fret. Merely place them close to the pond in an open children's wading pool or anything that can substitute for it, add some fertilizer to the water and drop in your few pieces of duckweed. If the water is warm (above 72°F.), the duckweed should start reproducing immediately and in a few weeks will cover the surface of the wading pool. Then you can dump the plants into the pond and consider that the plants will be there forever. Even though these are warmth-loving plants, they often come back in the late Spring/early Summer. The duckweeds of the genus *Lemna* have

Salvinia natans.

Salvinia auriculata.

Marsilea hirsuta

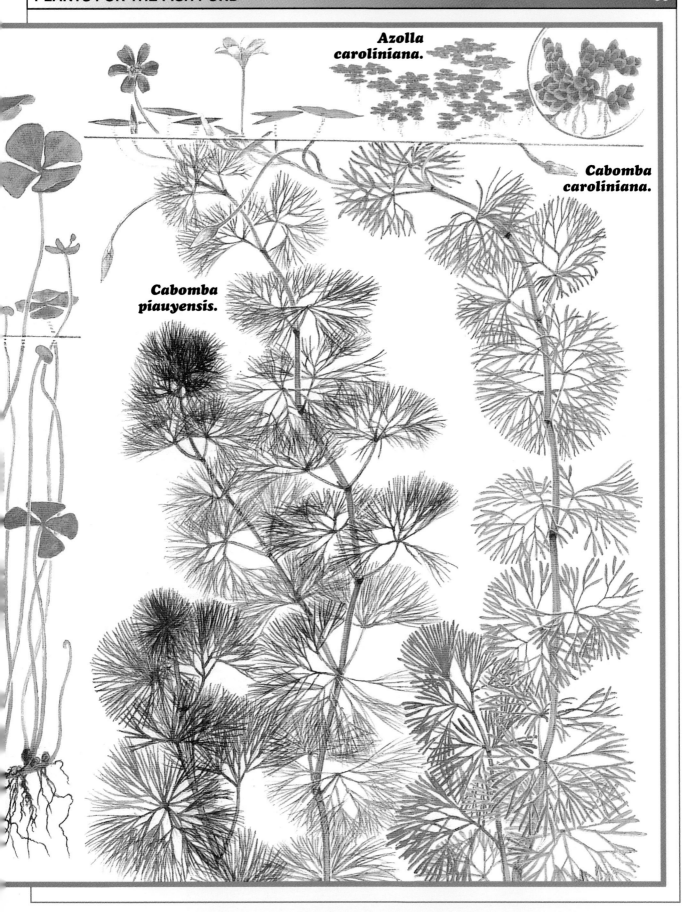

Azolla caroliniana.

Cabomba caroliniana.

Cabomba piauyensis.

minute flowers under ideal conditions. They have a single stamen and pistil, but no corolla. *Lemna* has a single small root.Very similar plants belong to the genera *Wolffia* and *Azolla*. It doesn't really matter which of these small floating plants you get. They all add the same lush green carpeting to your pond. They all have a single danger however.

Ponds breathe through their surface. The trapped gases, like the carbon dioxide produced by the fishes and the various gases produced by the rotting vegetation on the bottom of the pond, all escape from the pond in tiny bubbles which rise to the surface of the pond and are released into the atmosphere. The same is true of oxygen produced by the submerged plants. Fishes, by the way, can die from *gas bubble disease* when the bubbles of the super-saturated oxygen attach to their sticky gills.

For this reason you should not allow the surface of your pond to be completely covered with floating plants. A simple, effective cure is to place a huge aerator stone in the middle of your pond. By allowing it to bubble continuously, the turbulence will always keep a large area free of the floating plants. It will also assist the pond in ridding itself of noxious gases which accumulate on the bottom, and it will help to suppress water stratification. This means that the temperature in the pond will be more uniform regardless of the depth at which you measure the

water temperature. Normally, the top of a pond is more similar to the temperature of the surrounding air than is the bottom.

WATER HYACINTH

Unquestionably, the water hyacinth, *Eichhornia crassipes*, is the fastest growing pond plant. Under ideal conditions it doubles in size every week, requiring constant weeding. The plant is found throughout the world in tropical and sub-tropical climates. Huge floating mats of water

hyacinth clog up streams and ponds from Florida to Brazil.During one of his annual expeditions to Brazil, the author taught the local jungle people to collect the water hyacinth and boil it. The resulting *stew* is suitable as pig feed.

The water hyacinth serves many functions in the fish pond. In early Spring, its long tangles of roots serve as a safe area for koi and goldfish eggs. It also keeps the pond cool by shading a good section from the sun. Because it is so fast growing, it has to obtain as much

**Water Hyacinth,
Eichhornia crassipes.
Drawings from Holger
Windelov's Tropica
Catalogue.**

nutrition as possible from the water. In its efforts to take nutrients from the water it also takes toxic pollutants. Heavy metals accumulate in ponds because the water brought to the pond evaporates, leaving the heavy metals behind in the remaining water. Water hyacinths are known to absorb many heavy metals such as copper, lead, zinc and mercury.

There is no secret about planting water hyacinths; merely drop them onto the surface of the pond ensuring that they float right-side up. If the fishes in the pond are very hungry they will eat the roots of the water hyacinth and inhibit its prolific growth. Given full sunshine and water temperatures above 74°F., the plants double in size every week or ten days. The individual plants don't become larger, but they produce runners and each runner develops into a duplicate of the mother plant.

The water hyacinth frequently flowers...and just as frequently doesn't. Flowers may appear when the water reaches 72°F. The flowering phase ceases when temperatures drop below that at the end of the Summer.

Excess water hyacinths, as well as most of the plants growing in your pond, are easily sold to your local aquarium shop or garden center where koi and other pond fishes are sold. They like to buy local plants because they then are assured that these plants thrive under local weather conditions. Don't expect them to buy your plants at Summer's end.

ELODEA CANADENSIS

Elodea canadensis is almost a catch-all scientific name for all the temperate zones' *Elodea* and *Anacharis* species.

Though *Elodea* originates in Canada, it is now found throughout the temperate, tropical and sub-tropical world. In most countries the leaf shapes may vary from the norm...and some are very, very attractive. The author found some of what are called *Elodea crispa* in South Africa. Bringing the plants home, with their tightly curled leaves, he was very disappointed that they refused to grow in the pond. Placing a few strands in the aquarium didn't help much either. Obviously there was a water problem, with the water in South Africa differing from the water in New Jersey to such a degree that growth was retarded.

Visit your local pet shop and buy some LOCALLY GROWN *Elodea* or *Anacharis* if possible. Usually the *Elodea* is sold as a bunch plant with a rubber band or lead wire holding the bunch together. Unless these were grown locally, they will probably have been of tropical origin and will simply fall apart. If you can find some that have rooted in a small plastic pot, those are the ones to buy.

Once successfully rooted in your pond, they will grow in dense masses and be ideal for spawning goldfish and koi. Not only are they egg hideaways, but the newborn fry obtain maximum protection amongst their dense leaves.

Successful harvests of

Elodea can be sold on a regular basis to your local pet shop.

This plant is really not a floating plant as it does root in the soil. But in most ponds, the bunches are simply thrown into the pond and the *Elodea (=Anacharis)* floats, getting as much direct sunshine as possible.

CABOMBA AND MYRIOPHYLLUM

There are dozens if not hundreds of suitable plants for your fish pond. *Elodea (=Anacharis)*, though it roots, is usually found floating in ponds. The same is true of the various species of *Cabomba* and *Myriophyllum*. While these plants can be rooted, they are often sold in bunches and the bunches are usually unceremoniously dumped into the pond. Their prime purposes include a place for the eggs and a hiding place for the fry. They basically have no other function since they are always underwater, are always green and are quite unspectacular when viewed from above. Viewing them from the side in an aquarium is a different story. In an aquarium they serve many decorative functions which are not apparent in a pond.

For many years the author raised *Cabomba* and *Myriophyllum* in his pond. It would be harvested every week, bound in bunches with a rubber band, and sold to the local aquarium shop. The income from these plants, plus a few hundred water hyacinths, paid for all the expenses for food, filtration, water and electricity for a whole year.

MARGINAL PLANTS

Obviously, almost any plant which grows in your climate can be classified as a marginal plant. All you have to do is plant it alongside your fish pond. The garden center will usually have a hundred different kinds of marginal plants; and they probably have catalogues full of other attractive, flowering plants. The wisest way to decorate the ground around your fish pond is to get the advice of a gardener or architect who specializes in flowering plants, shrubs and bushes. Be sure to get a LOCAL expert. The author, for example, lives along the New Jersey shore. The trees, shrubs, bushes and flowering plants which thrive close to the Atlantic Ocean are not the same as those which thrive 500 feet away.

The most popular plant which is used universally as a margin plant is the iris. Known scientifically as *Iris siberica, Iris pseudoacorus, Iris ensata,* or any of a dozen other names, most of which are invalid, they are found in many colors and shapes. They are purchased as tubers and as they grow, they become massive clumps. The clumps must be separated every 3-5 years, so they must be dug up to be separated, of course. Planting is simple. The most hardy of the species if the familiar blue flowered *Iris siberica.* This can take freezing, but does better if some protection is afforded it. Usually a six inch covering of mulch will do the job well.

Iris siberica, found in blue or white and various shades in between, does best if planted in very shallow water

Otellia alismoides.

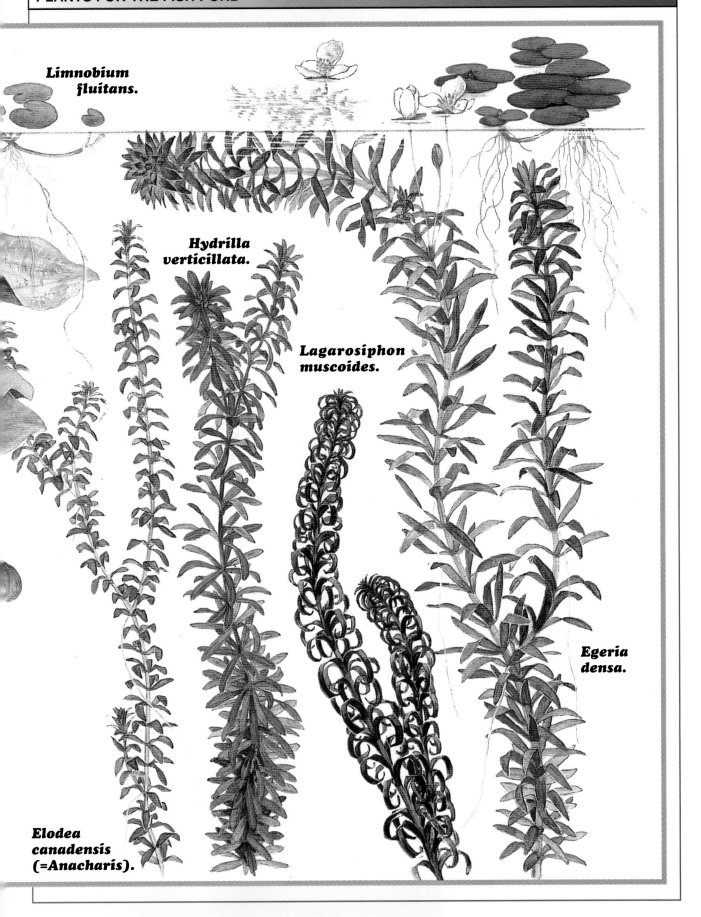

Limnobium fluitans.

Hydrilla verticillata.

Lagarosiphon muscoides.

Egeria densa.

Elodea canadensis (=Anacharis).

Above: **Beautiful purple Iris called *Iris* jerry. Photo by Leeann Connelly.** *Below:* **Yellow-white irises called *Iris* Dixie Deb. Photo by Leeann Connelly.**

in the fish pond. If you have no shallows, plant them in a large pot which will reach within a few inches of the surface of the pond. They should not be buried deeper than 3 inches in soil, nor deeper than 4 inches of water. They can also be planted in very wet soil. They die in normal dry soils unless they are thoroughly watered and never allowed to dry out.

Instructions for planting come with every package of *Iris* bulbs. Be sure to ask for WATER IRISES **when you buy irises from people unfamiliar with water gardens.**

The water irises originated in northern Eurasia, thus the scientific designation of *siberica* (Siberia).

LOTUS

The lotus is almost a sacred flower in many Oriental countries. It symbolizes beauty and honesty. Its flowers are extremely pretty and many Oriental girls have been named *Lotus Blossom* the way Western girls might be named *Rose* or *Iris.*

As a pond plant it has many advantages. Its leaves are huge and can be as large as three feet in diameter. It rises out of the water well over six feet, and it flowers for four months...the four summer months (June through September in New Jersey).

The lotus, scientifically known as *Nelumbo*, was originally cultivated in Ceylon (now Sri Lanka). The scientific name *Nelumbo* means *lotus blossom* in Sinhalese, the original language of Ceylon. Scientists used this name to describe the flower even though the rules require the scientific name to be Latin or Greek. There are different species of lotus found all over the world including North America and Australia. It does not occur naturally in South America, but it has been introduced there and is found in pockets in the rain forest of Amazonas State in Brazil.

The lotus reproduces by rhizomes. The rhizomes can be thought of as potatoes, and they should be planted in a horizontal position in soft, rich potting soil at a depth of 18 inches. They should be planted at the beginning of Spring (March in New Jersey). The rhizomes are delicate and are easily damaged with rough handling.

These are fast growing plants which are very aggressive when their conditions are right and they are fertilized (naturally or artificially). In full sunlight they flower and grow at tremendous speeds and have to be cut back continually or they will take over the pond. Get specific planting instructions from the garden center where you bought the rhizomes as there are three major species which require different handling. Lotus are NOT related to water lilies.

The plants which I have selected as examples are a very small sampling of plants which are actually available. The decision as to which plants are best for your fish pond should be made between you (for money and aesthetic decisions) and your landscape architect or gardener (who has water pond experience).

Above: **White Irises called *Iris* Marie Delores. Photo by Leeann Connelly. *Below:* A magnificent water garden. Photo by Leeann Connelly.**

Tropical Pond & Garden

Above: A view of the water gardens at Denver Botanic Gardens. Photo by Joseph V. Tomocik. Below: *Nelumbo* **'Perry's Giant Sunburst' is an outstanding new yellow lotus from Perry Slocum. Photo by Joseph V. Tomocik.**

Fishes for the Garden Pond

There is nothing more thrilling for a gardener than to have a living, moving garden. One in which the scene changes from moment to moment. The great French artist Monet drew dozens of paintings (now worth in the millions) of a single water garden featuring water lilies and the reflections of the sun on the water's surface. Often he could only paint an hour a day because the sun had to be in the same position for him to capture the glory of a shimmering water garden. As great as Monet was, he missed the ultimate glory of a garden pond with living jewels of different colors. Water lilies are beautiful...but you can't have them poke in your hand for food! Water lilies come in a dozen colors, fishes can be maintained in your garden pond with thousands or more colors.

The number of fishes and variety of species is determined by your pocketbook, climate, pond size and knowledge of fishes. A well managed garden pond can produce thousands of excess fishes and plants. These can easily be sold through local aquarium shops to make your pond cost-free.

There are two categories of fishes suitable for your water garden, just as there are two types of water lilies. The coldwater fishes are led by the Japanese colored carp, nishikigoi, which most westerners call KOI. Closely following the koi are the GOLDFISH. These two groups of fishes represent more than 90% of the fish populations found in water gardens in temperate zones. In the tropics, almost any fishes which are compatible can be kept. These fishes are called tropical fishes. Many books have been written about goldfish, koi and tropical fishes. (The present author has written almost 100 books on these fishes!) Local fishes, found in the streams and ponds, lakes and rivers in your own neighborhood, might also make useful additions to your garden pond but they will probably have several drawbacks. Usually most wild-caught fishes have little contrasting color, so they are almost invisible in your garden pond. Then, again, they might be too small or grow too large. Often they are predatory (catfish) and

The masterpiece by Claude Monet entitled *THE WATER LILY POND*.

The Claude Monet painting of the water lily pond at sunset.

nocturnal, so you almost never see them. The best advice, then, is to concentrate on koi and goldfish for your fish pond. In the summer, you can add Black Mollies, Red Swordtails, Gold Platies and perhaps some fancy guppies. Mollies come in gold, green and mottled, with Liberty Mollies even having some red in the tail. Albino Mollies are reddish yellow. Swordtails come in many colors and color combinations. Yellow, red, black, gold and combinations of these colors. They also have interesting fins with some of the very fancy varieties and some are called Hi-fin Swordtails. The same variations are found in platies. Visit your pet shop and become acquainted with the possibilities. Since these tropical fish are so small, you'll want to buy a substantial number of them to make a visual impact in your pond.

Put them into the pond when the water reaches over 70°F. Remove them when the water begins to drop below 70°F. Removing fishes from a water garden is never easy. The best way is to trap them. Small traps, often called *killie* traps, are made of plastic. They have a hole at each end (usually). Food is put into the traps to attract the fishes. The size of the hole determines the size of the fish which can enter the trap. These fishes are staples at your local aquarium shop. If possible, only buy pregnant females. One male can usually impregnate 100 females. Once impregnated, the tropical fishes mentioned above can deliver at least

Above: Black Sailfin Molly, *Poecilia latipinna*. This is a male and is suitable for the garden pond as long as temperatures stay 68°F. or higher. Photo by the author.

Above: Red Hifin Wagtail Platy, *Xiphophorus maculatus*. This is a male. They are suitable for the garden pond as long as temperatures stay above 68°F. Photo by the author.

Above: A Red Swordtail female staring to change sex into a non-functional male. These fish do well in the water garden as long as temperatures are about 70°F. Photo by the author.

At the very bottom of this photo a small red canister is, in reality, a heater. The pump (fountain) keeps the warmer water distributed throughout the pond and it stays free of ice, keeping the fishes alive. Photo by Dr.Burt Frank.

Goldfish can be trained to eat from your fingers. Photo by Michael Gilroy.

inbred that there is discussion about where the original goldfish came from. We do know that China and Japan have produced most of the weird goldfish varieties. Many of the new varieties are so monstrous as to be unable to survive in a garden pond. The Water Bubble-eye, for example, has huge sacs attached to the bases of its eyes which are so heavy that the goldfish can barely lift its head off the bottom. Then there is the Lionhead whose growth of tissue covers its head until its eyes are covered too! Goldfish which have long, flowing fins might not be able to compete for food, but many goldfish such as the Comet, Shubunkins, and Commons, are excellent.

The goldfish which should not be kept in garden ponds are the Veiltail, Fantail, Moor, Celestial, Bubble-eye, Pompons, Lionhead, Oranda, Pearlscale and Gill Curls.

Many fancy goldfish are illustrated in this book and their captions indicate their pluses and minuses. All goldfish have one great advantage over any other colorful pond fish...they eat as long as the water isn't frozen. Koi, on the other hand, usually stop feeding when the pond temperature reaches about 50°F.

four batches of fry, about one batch per month. These fishes, by the way, deliver their young alive. They are called *livebearers*.

GOLDFISH

Goldfish are the most popular of all pet fishes. They have been kept in homes for hundreds of years. So carefully have they been

Above: **Red-cap Oranda goldfish. Usually not suited for the outdoor water garden. Photo by Edward Taylor.**

Above: **Red Lionhead goldfish. Usually not suited for the outdoor water garden. Photo by Edward Taylor.**

Above: **Orange-and-black Telescope-eyed goldfish. Usually not suitable for the outdoor water garden. Photo by Fred Rosenzweig.** *Below:* **A common Comet goldfish. Perfectly suited for the outdoor water garden. Photo by Michael Gilroy.**

Above: **Red-and-white Pearlscale goldfish. Usually not suitable for the outdoor water garden. Photo by Edward Taylor.** *Below:* **Red-and-white Pompon Oranda goldfish. Usually not suitable for the outdoor water garden. Photo by Fred Rosenzweig.**

Above: A Celestial goldfish. Not suitable for the garden pond. Photo by Michael Gilroy.

Below: A Black Moor goldfish. Usually not suitable for the outdoor pond. Photo by the author.

Below: A Water Bubble-eye goldfish. Definitely not suitable for the outdoor pond. Photo by Ruda Zukal.

NISHIKIGOI, KOI

The original koi derived from the natural species *Cyprinus carpio*. There is considerable argument about exactly where it came from within central Europe, or from east Asia, as both ranges are recognized by subspecies. *Cyprinus carpio haematopterus* is found in eastern Asia where it may have been introduced 500 years ago. The European carp, *Cyprinus carpio carpio*, has a fascinating history which is discussed fully in *The Completely Illustrated Guide to Koi for Your Pond* written by Axelrod, Balon, Hoffman, Rothbard and Wohlfarth. While Europeans may have been the first to cultivate this fish, their interest was only food. It was the Chinese who recognized that the carp developed color abnormalities

Above: Koi are excellent pond fish because they are hardy, large, colorful and available in many colors. They are also excellent as food. Photo courtesy of Takeshi Yokoyama.

Below: *Cyprinus carpio*, the ancestor of the nishikigoi (koi). This fish still thrives in many countries around the world. Photo by Aqua Press, MP & C Piednoir.

Japanese carp streamers at Beppu. These streamers are called *koinobori* in Japanese. Photo by Roloff Beny.

Some koi reach 30 inches in total length (including the tail). The Japanese value large sized koi. Photo by Hugh Nicholas.

and they began to breed the fish for color and as a decoration for the garden ponds. The Chinese colors were very modest, though they were very attractive when compared to the dull colors of the wild carp.

Then along came the Japanese! When carp were first brought to Japan is not certain, but hundreds of years ago the Japanese used the carp as a model of determination, hardiness and good behavior and they lectured their children on *acting like a carp*. They have lovely streamers depicting koi (carp) which they fly from long poles in front of their houses to proclaim that their child was successful at getting into a university. The ultimate proclamation was the big C, a white letter against a crimson background that signified their favorite baseball team called the CARPS. The author was discussing this with a few baseball enthusiasts one night in Tokyo and very defensively they said:"*Hey, you have Dodgers, Giants, Braves and God knows what else. We'd rather be called a carp than a dodger*" That was the end of the conversation!

There are at least 13 color varieties of carp in Japan. These are recognized by most Japanese carp societies. There are many more color varieties which are not recognized in Japan. While the Japanese recognize colors which THEY created, they do not recognize colors which they did not create, nor do they recognize koi with elongated fins because they were not created in Japan!

In most koi societies around the world, the Japanese names for the color varieties are utilized. The Japanese, by the way, use American terms for their avid embrace of baseball in Japan. So we're even.

Beside the 13 or more categories of color varieties recognized by the Japanese, there can be as many as 20 size groupings and age groupings. The more koi entered into a show, the more categories. Thus, a Kohaku, the favorite red and white koi of Japan, can win a prize by color and by size, as well as by age.

All koi must be uniformly streamlined, with perfect fins. Only females, heavy with eggs, are forgiven their misshapen bodies. Permanent shortness, fatness or elongated or shortened fins are not acceptable in Japanese competitions.

COLOR VARIETIES OF KOI

With some color varieties, it is difficult to describe them. The wonderful photographs and the accompanying captions more than serve to assure you can identify the fish you have according to color.

Kohaku

While Kohaku are described as a white fish with red markings, it is also the most common color variety found in Japan. It almost always wins BEST IN SHOW prizes and while average specimens are very cheap, great specimens are very expensive. Judging Kohaku by color alone is not enough. The judges also consider the way the fish moves about,

This Kohaku koi won the grand prize in the adult carp division of the great Tokyo koi show. It is owned by Mr.Natsuiji Anabuki of Kagawa, Japan.

This Taisho-sanke, a three-colored carp, won grand prize in the great Tokyo show.

swims and uses its fins. When they look at the location of the red on the white body, they fantasize about it. I'm sure a psychologist would understand the meanings of these fantasies more than a fish lover.

Taisho-sanke

This is a three-colored fish. It actually is a Kohaku with black as a minor added color. The black must never be more highlighted than the red. The head must always have red. For a good specimen, the head should have more than 50% of it covered with a bright red.

Showa-sanshoku

This is a three-colored fish. Red, white and black, the same three colors which are characteristic of the Taisho-sanke. But the dominant color is black and this variety is referred to as a black fish with red and white markings. Most Japanese judges seem to favor a fish which is like a Kohaku but with about 25% black on is body and black in its pectoral fins.

Bekko

This is a simple two-colored fish. One of the colors must be black. The other color can be anything as long as it is solid. The black should be fingerprint-size on a fish of 24 inches in length. Some bekko are quite striking. Usually the term *bekko* is preceded by the Japanese name of another color to show the base coloration of the fish. Thus Shiro-bekko is a white fish (*shiro* means *white*) with black splashes randomly highlighting the fish's body.

This Showa-sanshoku is a three-colored fish which features intense black. This koi took the Grand Prize for males at the Tokyo great show.

Below: This is an Utsurimono of championship status.

Above: The two-colored, black and white, Bekko. This is a champion.

Utsurimono

This is a two-colored fish, the same as the Bekko, but the amount of black is of major importance. Theoretically if you take a Bekko (a fish which is less than 10% black) and compare it to an Utsurimono, you would consider the Utsurimono as a black fish with a second color. Generally speaking the black is about 25% of the fish's body color. Like the Bekko, the term *utsurimono* is preceded by an adjective which denotes the second color, thus a Shiro-utsurimono is a black and white fish.

Asagi shusui

These are two kinds of fish. They were the first of the fancy koi to appear in Japan, having been brought in from Germany at the end of the 19th Century. Because they were German and easily recognized by their lack of scales, they were called *Doitsu* which is the way the Japanese pronounced *Deutsch* (*deutsch* means *german* in the German language). The Germans are said to have favored these scaleless fish because they were easier to clean before eating.In any case, the Asagi are characterized by scales which have white edges around each one of them giving the fish a net-like appearance. An intense red covers the belly, the extended pectoral fins and the sides of the face (gill covers) and lips. The Shusui only have large, abnormal scales along the lateral line on the fish's sides, or along the back.

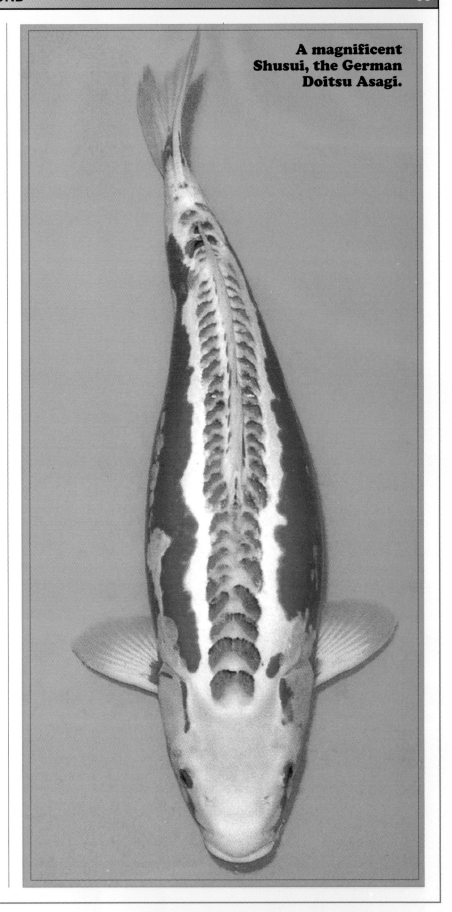

A magnificent Shusui, the German Doitsu Asagi.

Below: An Asagi champion.

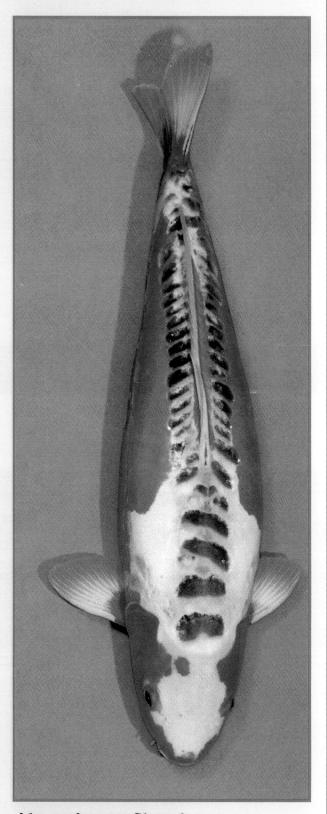

Above: A great Shusui.

Koromo

Where the Asagi have white edges to their scales, the Koromo have darker center which give the appearance of being blue. Though they are called *blue*, they are not blue at all. Just light black or gray. What happens is that the fish is basically a yellow fish with the black pigment missing from a wild-colored green fish. There are patches of another color, usually red, which, when the darker scales imprints upon them, give the scale a blue cast. Think of the fish as a Kohaku with a yellow body instead of a white one. Red blotches are highlighted with the darkness caused by the three colors.

In this variety, the netting must not impair the head.

Ogon

These are very interesting carp. They have a distinct metallic shine to their scales. This is exciting because they stand out so well against the normal black background offered by most fish ponds. The usual colors are platinum, white or gold. They are very popular with American water gardeners because of their low price and beauty.

The Ogon are a solid, single color.

Hikari-moyomono

This is an Ogon of more than one color. The term *hikari*, made famous by Shigezu Kamihata when he named his best-selling koi food Hikari, actually describes a flash of lightning. They can be of any recognized color.

A magnificent Koromo champion with magnificent brocading and blood red coloring.

**Below: The elusive Hikari-mugi. Not a
well known color variety.**

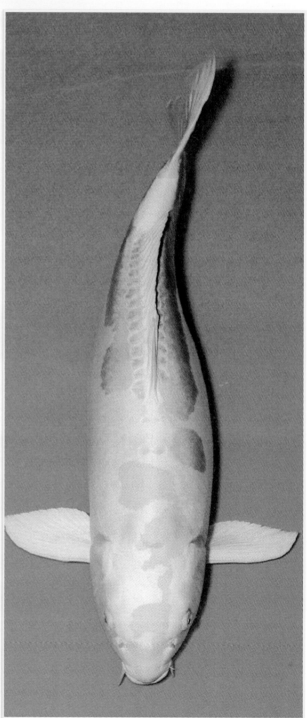

**Above: The Hikari-moyo. Not a well-
known color variety.**

Above: The Kinginrin. This Ogon (metallic scales) won a championship. This is a golden Ogon.

Below: This Ogon is a silver Ogon champion.

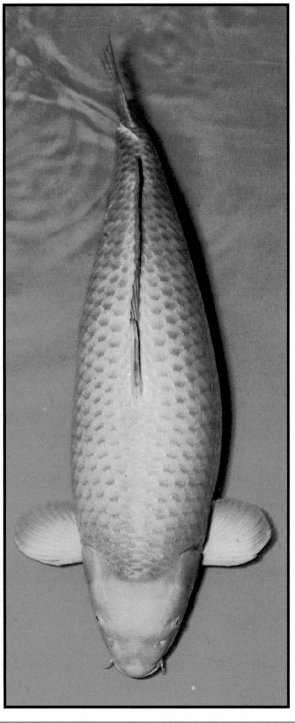

An Hikari-utsurimono of championship quality.

Hikari-utsurimono

The Utsurimono is a bi-colored fish whose major color is supposed to be black (but rarely is!). The black marking are very large, not thumb-print size. The Hikari-utsurimono is a metallic fish.

Kawarimono

Any attractive koi which does not conveniently fit into a recognized color pattern is called a *Kawarimono*. Most koi shows have such a class to encourage participation in the show and to get more entry fees. It is very VERY rare for a Kawarimono to win a Best-in-Show prize.

Kinginrin

This might well be the most attractive scalation found in koi. They exist in every color classification (though usually Kohaku is the most popular) and they feature very shiny scales which reflect the light in various directions as the fish swims. The scales are variously described as being silvery, reflective and/or metallic. Regardless of what they are called, when you see one, you'll never forget it. There are many categories of Kinginrin since basic coloration categories are enhanced with the ginrin scalation.

Tancho

The Japanese stork which has a red crown is called a *tancho*. The Japanese flag was the red rising sun against a white background. Thus do the Japanese have a special place in their hearts for bright red round markings. Any color variety of koi can have a red tancho

Below: A two-colored B-Kinginrin. The difference between the A and B is the *tsubu-gin* which is a pearl-like growth in the center of each scale. The B's have it; the A's do not.

Above: A three-colored A-Kinginrin of championship quality, though a very young fish.

mark on its head. The more perfect the circle, the more intense the color and the more contrasting with its background, determines the quality of the tancho.

Long-finned Koi

Bred in America, these magnificent koi have been condemned by the Japanese koi authorities as unfit for competition. This position is quickly losing support as the long-finned koi become available in more and more color varieties. Many are sold in pet shops as aquarium pets, besides their being ideal for the garden pond. More than half of the author's pond fish are long-finned koi.

Left: Magnificent long-finned (butterfly) koi developed in the U.S.A. and rejected in Japanese-sponsored koi shows because it is not of Japanese origin. This is a poor excuse. Photo by David LeFever of fish developed at Blue Ridge Fish Farms.

A very young butterfly, long-finned koi. Photo by Jim Stratford.

Below: A lovely Tancho which won the 1989 Tokyo koi show.

Above: A champion Hi-utsuri which won the 1989 Tokyo great show.

Showa-sanshoku.

Utsurimono.

Hikari-mugi.

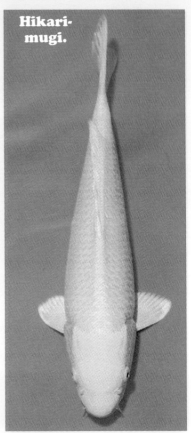

Hikari-moyo.

Asagi.

Shusui.

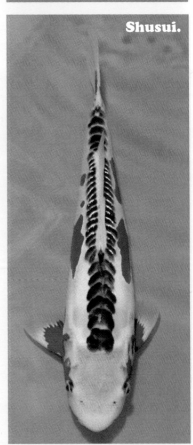

Goshiki.

Kawarimono.

A-Ginrin.

B-Ginrin.

Hikari-utsuri.

Tancho.

THESE KOI BOOKS ARE COMPLETELY ILLUSTRATED WITH MAGNIFICENT COLOR DRAWINGS AND PHOTOS. THEY ARE AVAILABLE THROUGH YOUR LOCAL PET SHOP.

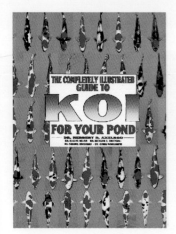

THE COMPLETELY ILLUSTRATED GUIDE TO KOI FOR YOUR POND
By Axelrod, Balon, Hoffman, Rothbard and Wohlfarth.
TS-268
This is the most modern, scientific, historical and complete book ever written about koi. If you don't buy it, at least read it. The authors call it the best book they have ever written.

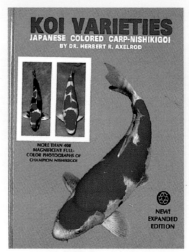

KOI VARIETIES
By Dr. Herbert R. Axelrod
PS-875
This colorful book covers the many varieties available, selection, and history of the increasingly popular Koi.
HC, 8 1/2 x 11" 144 pages, over 500 full color photos.
ISBN 0-866622-162-X
UPC 0-18214-28853-4

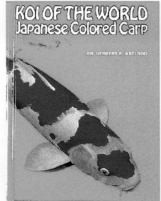

KOI OF THE WORLD
By Dr. Herbert R. Axelrod
H-947
This is the first large book ever written about koi. It has chapters of feeding, breeding, diseases, ponds, koi sales and shows, kinds and colors of koi, etc. It may be the most complete book on the subject. HC, 9 x 12" 239 pages, 327 full color photos.
ISBN 0-87666-092-8
UPC 0-18214-60928-5

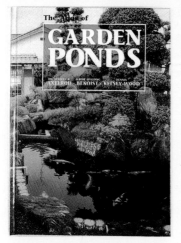

ATLAS OF WATER GARDENS
By Axelrod, Benoist and Kelsey-Wood.
TS-178
10x14", 272 pages, more than 300 colored drawings and photos. This book contains architectural layouts for garden ponds. It is all you need to know about successful water gardening.

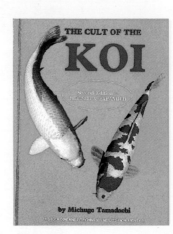

CULT OF THE KOI
By Michugo Tamadachi
TS-132
This book is big and beautiful, highly colorful and highly fascinating. This is the Bible for koi lovers. HC, 9 1/4 x 12 1/4" 288 pages, over 500 full color photos.
ISBN 0-866622-440-8
UPC 0-18214-20852-5